Homeland to Heartland

The Sindhi Migration Tale

Listen to the Voices, Feel the Pain, Learn the Lessons, and Carry the Flame

Dr Jahanavi V. Ahuja

Homeland to Heartland:
The Sindhi Migration Tale

Listen to the Voices, Feel the Pain,
Learn the Lessons, and

Carry the Flame

By:

Dr Jahanavi V. Ahuja

"O my land, you are my pride, my strength; even if I leave, my soul shall always reside in you."

Ustad Bukhari

Content

WHY THIS BOOK 5

THE UNBREAKABLE SPIRIT OF SINDHIS: A STORY OF MIGRATION, STRUGGLES, AND TRIUMPH 5

CHAPTER 1 8

THE LAND OF SINDH - GEOGRAPHICAL, CULTURAL, AND HISTORICAL SIGNIFICANCE..............8

CHAPTER 2...........................28

LIFE IN SINDH BEFORE PARTITION 28

CHAPTER 3............................37

THE CALL FOR PARTITION: POLITICAL TURMOIL AND RISING TENSIONS 37

CHAPTER 4............................47

THE ROLE OF WOMEN IN SINDHI SOCIETY 47

CHAPTER 5............................50

SINDH'S ECONOMIC AND BUSINESS LEGACY: THE ENTREPRENEURIAL SPIRIT OF SINDHIS 50

CHAPTER 6............................55

THE GREAT MIGRATION STORIES OF DEPARTURE AND HEARTBREAK.....55

CHAPTER 7............................67

CONCLUSION: THE EVERLASTING LEGACY OF SINDH.............................. 67

ABOUT AUTHOR 73

WHY THIS BOOK

The Unbreakable Spirit of Sindhis: A Story of Migration, Struggles, and Triumph

Partition of India in 1947 was not just a division of land but also the division of hearts, homes, and histories. Among the most affected communities were Sindhis, who were uprooted from their motherland and forced to migrate to an unknown future.

For centuries, Sindh was a thriving land, known for its rich culture, flourishing trade, and the spirit of unity among its people. Our ancestors-built businesses, homes, and institutions with their hard work and perseverance. However, in 1947, everything changed overnight. Sindhis, who had been an integral part of undivided India, were suddenly without a homeland. They left behind their wealth, homes, temples, and even the ashes of their ancestors, carrying only memories and hope.

Despite being displaced, Sindhis did not lose their determination. They started from scratch, working tirelessly to build a new life in India. From setting up small businesses on footpaths to establishing some of the biggest enterprises in the country today, the journey of Sindhis has been nothing short of inspiring. Their resilience, business acumen, and indomitable spirit transformed adversity into opportunity.

Yet, we often hear taunts that Sindhis came 'empty-handed' and are now living a luxurious life. This narrative overlooks the immense sacrifices and hardships that our grandparents and great-grandparents endured. No one handed success to Sindhis on a platter. Every penny earned was through sweat and sacrifice. Every achievement was built on sleepless nights and tireless work.

Sindhis did not just survive; they thrived. But at no point did we forget our roots. We remained patriotic Indians, contributing to the growth and prosperity of the nation. We carried forward the values of our ancestors—hard work, honesty, and resilience. Today, Sindhis are among the most respected business leaders, entrepreneurs, and professionals in India. Our success is a testament to our spirit, not a stroke of luck.

To those who question our place in India, let us remind them: we were Indian before the partition, we are Indian today, and we will always be Indian. Our history is deeply intertwined with this land, and our contribution to India's economy, culture, and society is undeniable.

The story of Sindhi migration is not just about displacement but about courage, determination, and the will to rise again. It is a reminder that no matter how difficult the circumstances, a community united by values and hard work will always find its way to success.

We are Sindhi. We are Indian. And we will always be proud of both.

Chapter 1

The Land of Sindh - Geographical, Cultural, and Historical Significance

"Sindh is not just land; it is a melody, a poem, a love that never fades."

Shaikh Ayaz

Meera clutched the edge of her dupatta, her heart pounding as she stood on the deck of the ship that carried her away from Sindh. The gentle waves of the Arabian Sea rocked the vessel, a rhythm that once brought comfort but now felt like an unsettling farewell. She turned back one last time, hoping to catch a glimpse of the land she had called home—the land that held the golden sands of Thar, the bustling markets of Karachi, the serene banks of the Indus, and the whispered prayers from Sufi shrines. But all she could see was the endless expanse of water stretching between her past and her uncertain future.

She was not alone. With her stood her mother-in-law, a woman of quiet resilience who had spent her entire life in Sindh, now forced to leave everything behind. Her husband, a man determined to carve out a new life in India, stood beside her, trying to mask his own anxieties under the weight of responsibility. Two brothers-in-law, still young and impressionable, stared at the sea with a mixture of excitement and fear. And then there was her sister-in-law, her husband's younger sister, who, like Meera, had left behind childhood memories, dear friends, and the familiarity of home.

The journey was not easy. The ship was crowded with families like hers—men, women, and children who had carried with them nothing but a few belongings and an immeasurable sense of loss. Meera held onto a small bundle wrapped in cloth, which contained a handful of Sindhi soil her mother had secretly placed in her hands before she left. It was the last tangible connection to her homeland.

Her mind wandered back to the home she had left behind—the courtyard where she used to sit with her mother, listening to stories of their ancestors, the smell of freshly cooked Sindhi Saag wafting through the air, the vibrant celebrations of Cheti Chand where the entire neighborhood would come together. Those memories, now distant, felt like treasures slipping through her fingers.

Her mother-in-law sat beside her, silent but lost in thought. Meera knew she was remembering her ancestral home, the house where generations had lived, laughed, and loved. She had spent years raising her children within its walls, believing that they would continue to do the same. But fate had other plans. Meera reached for her hand and gave it a gentle squeeze. It was all they could do—hold onto each other as they sailed into an unknown future.

As the ship moved forward, Meera observed the other passengers. Some were whispering prayers, others were in tears, and some simply sat in a daze, unable to comprehend the magnitude of what was happening. The children, unaware of the depth of the situation, played in small corners of the deck, their laughter an ironic contrast to the sorrow surrounding them.

The sun was beginning to set, casting an orange glow over the waves. Meera's husband sat beside her and finally spoke, his voice filled with quiet resolve. "We will build a new life, Meera. We will make a home again."

She nodded, though a lump formed in her throat. Home. The word felt different now. It was no longer a place but a feeling—a collection of stories, traditions, and people who carried Sindh in their hearts.

She wiped her tears and looked at the sky. Perhaps, just like the sun that had set behind her, a new dawn awaited them across the sea. As Meera's ship sailed further away, she whispered a silent promise—to keep the essence of Sindh alive in her new world, to pass down its stories, its songs, and its spirit to the generations yet to come.

The land of Sindh

"The fragrance of Sindh's soil speaks of devotion, where love flows like a river, unchained and free."

Sami (Syed Mir Ali)

Geographical Significance of Sindh

Sindh, located in the southeastern part of Pakistan, is a land shaped by the mighty Indus River. The river, known as the lifeline of Sindh, has nurtured civilizations for thousands of years, bringing fertility to its plains and sustaining human settlements. To the west, the Kirthar Range stands as a silent guardian, while the Thar Desert in the east stretches into India, creating a striking contrast between arid lands and fertile fields.

The province's coastal belt, with its bustling ports such as Karachi and Keti Bandar, has historically served as a gateway for traders, travelers, and conquerors. Sindh's strategic location made it a bridge between South Asia and the Middle East, influencing its culture, trade, and politics over centuries.

Cultural Significance of Sindh

Sindh is a land of diversity, where ancient traditions blend seamlessly with contemporary life. The Sindhi language, with its lyrical poetry and rich folklore, echoes in the streets and countryside, carrying tales of love, loss, and devotion. The land has produced some of the greatest Sufi poets, such as Shah Abdul Latif Bhittai, Sachal Sarmast, and Lal Shahbaz Qalandar, whose verses transcend religious and social barriers, promoting harmony and universal love.

The Sindhi people take immense pride in their vibrant festivals, such as Cheti Chand, the Sindhi New Year, and Urs celebrations at Sufi shrines, where music and dance create an atmosphere of spiritual ecstasy. Traditional attire, such as the Ajrak and Sindhi topi, is not just a fashion statement but a symbol of cultural identity and historical pride.

Sindh's cuisine, enriched by the flavors of its land and sea, tells the story of its people. From the spicy Sindhi Biryani to the comforting Sai Bhaji (a lentil and spinach dish), every meal carries the essence of centuries-old culinary traditions, blending indigenous ingredients with Persian and Central Asian influences.

Historical Significance of Sindh

The history of Sindh is as deep and layered as the Indus itself. It is home to one of the oldest civilizations in the world—the Indus Valley Civilization—where cities like Mohenjo-daro thrived over 4,500 years ago. These ancient urban centers boasted remarkable advancements in architecture, drainage systems, and trade, showcasing an early sophistication that still fascinates historians and archaeologists.

Sindh's history has been shaped by waves of invaders and settlers, from the Aryans and Persians to the Arabs and British. The most defining moment came in 711 AD when Muhammad bin Qasim, an Arab general, conquered Sindh, bringing Islam to the region. This event marked the beginning of a new cultural synthesis, blending Hindu and Buddhist traditions with Islamic influences.

During the colonial era, Sindh was annexed by the British in 1843, leading to economic and infrastructural changes but also resistance movements that fought for self-rule. The partition of India in 1947 altered Sindh's demographic fabric, with a significant exodus of Sindhi Hindus to India and the arrival of Muslim migrants from across the border. This shift, which Meera and her family were part of, left an indelible mark on the history and identity of Sindh.

Sindh in Modern Times

Today, Sindh stands as a province rich in culture and economic potential. Karachi, its capital, is Pakistan's economic hub, a city of contrasts where skyscrapers rise beside colonial-era buildings, and bustling markets coexist with modern shopping centers. The rural heartlands of Sindh continue to cherish age-old traditions, where farming communities thrive along the banks of the Indus, and Sufi shrines draw thousands seeking solace and blessings.

Despite facing challenges such as climate change, water scarcity, and urbanization, Sindh remains resilient, much like Meera and countless others who carried a piece of their homeland in their hearts. Whether in the melodies of Sindhi songs, the aroma of home-cooked meals, or the enduring spirit of its people, Sindh lives on— forever etched in the soul of those who have called it home.

The Vibrant Life and Traditions of Sindhi Families

Sindhi families are known for their deep-rooted traditions, cultural richness, and warm hospitality. Whether in Sindh, Pakistan, or across the Sindhi diaspora worldwide, they have maintained their customs while embracing modernity. The essence of a Sindhi household is characterized by strong family bonds, festive celebrations, delicious cuisine, and a profound respect for spiritual and social values.

Family Structure and Values

Sindhi families have traditionally been joint families, where multiple generations live under one roof. This system fosters a strong sense of unity, respect, and mutual care. While nuclear families have become more common in modern times, the values of respect for elders, collective decision-making, and close familial ties remain intact.

Respect for elders is an integral part of Sindhi culture. Parents and grandparents are held in high esteem, and their guidance is considered crucial in important matters, including education, marriage, and financial decisions. Younger generations are taught to honor traditions and uphold the family's reputation through their actions and achievements.

Festivals and Celebrations

Festivals play a significant role in the lives of Sindhi families. They are occasions of joy, togetherness, and devotion. Some of the most prominent Sindhi festivals include:

- **Cheti Chand**: This marks the Sindhi New Year and celebrates the birth of **Jhulelal,** the deity of the Sindhi community. It is observed with grand processions, prayers, and community feasts.

- **Diwali and Holi**: For Sindhi Hindus, Diwali is a time for prayer, family gatherings, and lighting diyas, while Holi is celebrated with colors and joy.

- **Teejri**: A festival where Sindhi women fast and pray for the well-being of their husbands and families, similar to Karva Chauth.

- **Chaliyo**: A festival where sindhi people observe fast for 40 days and worship Jhulelal. They offer aarti, akkho, Pallav, and at last they distribute '**Sesa**' [sweet rice]. They feed aquatic animals, especially on Fridays.

These celebrations often involve traditional music, dance, and sumptuous feasts, bringing families and communities closer together.

Sindhi Cuisine: A Delight for the Senses

Food is a vital part of Sindhi culture, and Sindhi households take great pride in their culinary traditions. Sindhi cuisine is a delightful blend of flavours, with an emphasis on spices, seasonal vegetables, and slow-cooked delicacies. Some famous Sindhi dishes include:

- **Sai Bhaji**: A nutritious dish made with spinach, lentils, and vegetables.

- **Sindhi Kadhi**: A tangy gram flour-based curry with vegetables, served with rice.

- **Dal Pakwan**: A breakfast favorite consisting of crispy fried bread (pakwan) served with spiced lentils.

- **Aloo Tuk**: Sliced potatoes stir-fried with spices, often served as a side dish.

- **Seviyan (Vermicelli Kheer)**: A sweet dish made with milk and dry fruits, enjoyed during festivals and special occasions.

- **Dhodho Chutney**: It is a thick chapati made from different flours such as maize, jowar, bajra, rice etc added with veggies and spices and served with green chutney.

- **Behe patata**: It is an onion gravy dish which contains pieces of lotus stem and potatoes.

Sindhi families often gather around the dining table, sharing meals and stories, reinforcing the importance of togetherness in their culture.

Traditional Attire

The traditional attire of Sindhi families reflects their vibrant culture and heritage. Men often wear **Sindhi topis** (embroidered caps) along with shalwar kameez or kurta pajamas, while women adorn themselves in colorful **Ajrak**-printed dupattas, sarees, or shalwar kameez with intricate embroidery. The Ajrak, a traditional block-printed textile, holds deep cultural significance and is often gifted on special occasions.

On festive occasions and weddings, both men and women dress in elaborate and heavily embroidered outfits, showcasing the richness of Sindhi craftsmanship.

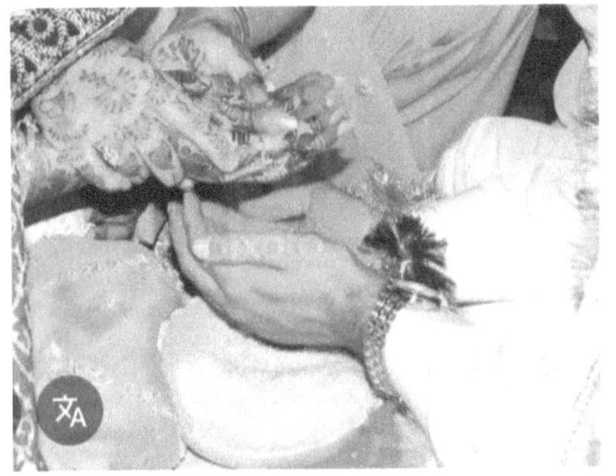

Marriage and Wedding Traditions

Sindhi weddings are grand and full of traditional rituals, symbolizing the sacred bond between two families. The celebrations last for several days and include:

- **Kachchi Misri**: A pre-engagement ceremony where families exchange sweets as a token of agreement.

- **Pakki Misri**: The formal engagement where rings are exchanged.

- **Mehendi and Sangeet**: Celebrations filled with music, dance, and the application of henna.

- **Behrana Sahib**: A prayer ceremony invoking the blessings of Sai Jhulelal.

- **Ghari Puja**: A ritual performed before the wedding to seek blessings from deities.

- **Sindhi Bhaan**: The bride is showered with gifts and jewellery before the wedding.

- **Wedding Ceremony**: Traditionally conducted as per Hindu customs, followed by grand feasts and celebrations.

Sindhi weddings are known for their lavish feasts, vibrant decorations, and joyous atmosphere where music and dance play a significant role.

Spiritual and Religious Beliefs

Sindhi families have deep spiritual roots and embrace diverse religious beliefs. Many Sindhis follow Hinduism and Islam, while some also practice Sikhism and other faiths. Devotion to **Jhulelal** is particularly strong among Sindhi Hindus, and his blessings are sought in every aspect of life.

Daily prayers, recitations, and religious gatherings are a common part of life, emphasizing peace, wisdom, and community service.

Art, Music, and Folklore

Sindhi families have a rich artistic heritage, with folk music and storytelling playing a crucial role in cultural expression. Traditional Sindhi music, featuring instruments like the **ektara**, **alghoza**, and **dhol**, is soulful and often accompanied by devotional singing known as **bhajans**.

Popular Sindhi folk dances include:

- **Chhej**: A group dance performed during celebrations.

- **Jhoomar**: A rhythmic dance that symbolizes joy and festivity.

Sindhi folklore is filled with tales of love, bravery, and wisdom. Stories of **Moomal-Rano**, **Sassui-Punnhun**, and **Dodo Chanesar** have been passed down through generations, keeping the cultural heritage alive.

Education and Professional Life

Education is highly valued in Sindhi families, with a strong emphasis on academic and professional success. Many Sindhis have excelled in business, medicine, engineering, law, and the arts. Sindhi entrepreneurs, in particular, have established thriving businesses worldwide, earning a reputation for their business acumen and resilience.

Parents encourage children to pursue higher education and professional careers, often supporting them in their entrepreneurial ventures. The spirit of hard work and perseverance is deeply ingrained in Sindhi culture.

Conclusion

Sindhi families embody a unique blend of tradition and modernity. While they cherish and uphold their cultural heritage, they also adapt to changing times with resilience and grace. Their strong familial bonds, joyous celebrations, rich cuisine, and deep spiritual roots make Sindhi culture one of the most vibrant in the world. Despite geographical distances, Sindhis continue to preserve their identity, passing down their traditions to future generations with love and pride.

Chapter 2

Life in Sindh Before Partition

Sindh, a province in present-day Pakistan, has a rich and diverse history that dates back thousands of years. Before the Partition of India in 1947, Sindh was a land of cultural, religious, and economic harmony, where people of different faiths and backgrounds coexisted. The region was known for its distinct Sindhi identity, which was deeply influenced by its geographical location, the mighty Indus River, and its connection to the Arabian Sea. Life in Sindh before Partition was characterized by vibrant social customs, economic prosperity, and a deep-rooted cultural and religious pluralism.

Social and Cultural Life

The social fabric of Sindh before Partition was woven with a spirit of coexistence and communal harmony. Hindus, Muslims, Sikhs, Parsis, Jains, and Christians lived together, often sharing social and religious spaces. The Sindhi identity was not defined strictly by religion but by a shared cultural heritage that included language, cuisine, folklore, and traditions.

1. Religious Harmony and Festivals

Sindh was home to a large Hindu population, which coexisted peacefully with Muslims and other communities. Hindus and Muslims participated in each other's festivals with enthusiasm. Hindus celebrated Diwali, Holi, and Navratri, while Muslims observed Eid and Muharram. The Urs (death anniversaries) of Sufi saints were grand occasions that attracted devotees from all communities. The shrine of Shah Abdul Latif Bhittai, Lal Shahbaz Qalandar, and other Sufi saints were revered by Hindus and Muslims alike.

2. Language and Literature

Sindhi was the common language spoken by people of all faiths. It had a rich literary tradition with poets like Shah Abdul Latif Bhittai, Sachal Sarmast, and Sami composing verses that emphasized love, devotion, and unity. The storytelling traditions and folk tales, such as those of **Sassui-Punnhun** and **Moomal-Rano**, were shared cultural treasures.

3. Education and Intellectual Life

Education was a vital part of Sindhi society. Many Sindhi Hindus were well-educated and contributed significantly to the fields of law, medicine, business, and administration. Prominent educational institutions like the D. J. Sindh College in Karachi provided quality education to students from different backgrounds. The presence of Persian, Arabic, and Sanskrit studies further enriched the intellectual landscape of Sindh.

Economic Life

Sindh was an economically prosperous region before Partition, with agriculture, trade, and craftsmanship forming the backbone of its economy.

1. Agriculture and Rural Life

The fertile lands along the Indus River provided abundant agricultural opportunities. Wheat, rice, cotton, sugarcane, and fruits like dates and mangoes were widely cultivated. The canal irrigation system, first developed under British rule, enhanced agricultural productivity. Rural

Sindhis, both Hindu and Muslim, engaged in farming, cattle-rearing, and fishing.

2. Trade and Commerce

Trade was a major aspect of Sindh's economy. Karachi, a rapidly growing port city, was a hub for international trade, connecting Sindh to Bombay (Mumbai), the Middle East, and beyond. Sindhi traders and businessmen, particularly the Hindu Baniya and Amil communities, played a crucial role in commerce. They dealt in textiles, spices, handicrafts, and banking, often extending financial services to different parts of India and abroad.

3. Crafts and Industries

Sindh was known for its craftsmanship. The traditional Sindhi Ajrak (block-printed shawl), Sindhi embroidery, lacquer work, and pottery were highly valued. Artisan communities thrived, producing handwoven fabrics, carpets, and jewelry. Cities like Hyderabad and Shikarpur were renowned for their bustling markets and skilled craftsmen.

Family and Community Life

Families in Sindh were deeply rooted in traditions and customs. Joint family systems were common, where multiple generations lived together under one roof. Elders were respected, and family decisions were made collectively. The roles of men and women were clearly defined, with men engaging in trade and agriculture, while women managed households and participated in crafts and religious activities.

Women, particularly in Hindu families, played an essential role in preserving cultural traditions. They performed religious rituals, sang folk songs, and engaged in social welfare activities. Muslim women, particularly in rural areas, often participated in agricultural work alongside men.

Religious and Philosophical Beliefs

Sindh's spiritual landscape was deeply influenced by Sufism, which promoted the ideals of love, tolerance, and unity. Sufi shrines, such as those of Shah Abdul Latif Bhittai, Lal Shahbaz Qalandar, and Sachal Sarmast, were visited by people from all religious backgrounds. These saints preached a message of oneness that transcended religious boundaries.

Hinduism in Sindh had a distinct flavor, with many followers of the Bhakti movement worshipping deities like Jhulelal, the patron saint of Sindhi Hindus. Temples and shrines dedicated to Krishna, Shiva, and Shakti were common, and many Hindu Sindhis followed a syncretic form of worship that incorporated Sufi influences.

Challenges and British Colonial Rule

Under British rule, Sindh underwent significant changes. The British annexed Sindh in 1843, introducing modern administrative systems, railways, and communication networks. While economic development improved, British policies also disrupted traditional industries and altered the socio-economic landscape.

1. Land Reforms and Economic Disparities

The British introduced land tenure systems that favored large landlords and feudal elites, often at the expense of small farmers. This created economic disparities and dependence on landlords.

2. Social Changes and Political Awakening

The British educational system brought Western ideas, leading to political awareness among Sindhis. The Indian National Congress and the Muslim League both had a presence in Sindh, and debates over self-rule and communal representation intensified in the years leading up to Partition.

Partition and Its Impact

The Partition of India in 1947 marked a tragic turning point in Sindh's history. While Sindh did not witness the large-scale violence seen in Punjab and Bengal, the social and demographic landscape changed drastically. Most Sindhi Hindus, who had been an integral part of Sindh's society and economy, were forced to migrate to India due to communal tensions and fear of persecution. This led to a massive loss of cultural heritage and economic expertise.

The departure of Sindhi Hindus left a void in trade, education, and administration. Their migration to India led to the formation of Sindhi communities in cities like Mumbai, Ahmedabad, and Jaipur, where they rebuilt their businesses and cultural institutions. Meanwhile, Sindh in Pakistan saw an influx of Muslim refugees (Muhajirs) from India, altering the region's demographics and social fabric.

Conclusion

Life in Sindh before Partition was a testament to cultural coexistence, economic prosperity, and a deep-rooted sense of identity. The land of the Indus was a melting pot of traditions, where people of different faiths lived in harmony. The tragedy of Partition disrupted this centuries-old way of life, leading to the displacement of Sindhi Hindus and the transformation of Sindh's social and economic landscape. However, the legacy of pre-Partition Sindh continues to live on in the memories of those who experienced it and in the cultural heritage preserved by Sindhis across the world.

Chapter 3

The Call for Partition: Political Turmoil and Rising Tensions

The demand for the partition of British India into two separate nations—India and Pakistan—was one of the most significant and controversial events of the 20th century. The roots of this demand lay in the socio-political and religious divisions that had existed in the subcontinent for centuries. However, it was in the late 19th and early 20th centuries that this division took on a political dimension, ultimately culminating in the violent and traumatic Partition of 1947. This document will explore the political turmoil, rising tensions, and early signs of displacement that signaled the impending division.

1. Background to the Demand for Partition

The idea of partition did not emerge overnight. It was the result of decades of political and religious friction, exacerbated by British colonial policies and the growing assertiveness of communal identities.

British Colonial Policies and Divide-and-Rule

The British employed a "divide-and-rule" policy to maintain control over the vast and diverse Indian subcontinent. They often pitted religious communities against one another to weaken nationalist movements. The implementation of separate electorates in the Indian Councils Act of 1909 institutionalized religious divisions by allowing Muslims to elect their own representatives separately from Hindus. This reinforced the idea that Hindus and Muslims had distinct political interests.

The Rise of Muslim Nationalism

The All-India Muslim League, founded in 1906, emerged as a political organization advocating for Muslim interests. Initially, the League sought protection within a united India but later shifted towards demanding a separate nation. The demand for Pakistan, formally articulated in the Lahore Resolution of 1940, was based on the argument that Hindus and Muslims constituted separate nations with distinct cultures, histories, and religious practices.

Hindu-Muslim Political Rivalry

The Indian National Congress, the dominant nationalist party, largely advocated for a united India. However, its failure to address Muslim concerns, coupled with growing communal tensions, led to increasing alienation. While leaders like Mahatma Gandhi and Jawaharlal Nehru sought unity, Muhammad Ali Jinnah and the Muslim League argued that Muslims would be politically marginalized in a Hindu-majority India.

2. Political Turmoil and Rising Tensions

The 1940s saw escalating political confrontations, civil unrest, and communal violence. Several key events set the stage for the eventual partition.

The Cripps Mission (1942)

The British, facing mounting pressure during World War II, sent Sir Stafford Cripps to negotiate with Indian leaders regarding self-governance. However, his proposals were rejected, exacerbating tensions between the Congress and the Muslim League.

The Quit India Movement (1942)

In 1942. The Indian National Congress launched the Quit India Movement, demanding an immediate end to British rule. The British responded with mass arrests and repression, while the Muslim League distanced itself from the movement. This further widened the rift between Hindus and Muslims.

Direct Action Day (1946)

One of the most significant turning points was Direct Action Day, declared by the Muslim

League on August 16, 1946, to assert its demand for
Pakistan. The day led to horrific communal riots in
Calcutta, leaving thousands dead. This sparked a
chain reaction of violence across the country,
deepening the animosity between communities.

The Interim Government and Breakdown of Unity

An interim government was formed in 1946,
with Congress and the Muslim League sharing
power. However, ideological clashes and mutual
distrust led to its failure, making partition seem
increasingly inevitable.

3. Early Signs of Displacement

As partition became a certainty, signs of
mass displacement began appearing. These
included migration patterns, economic disruptions,
and increased communal hostilities.

Mass Migration Begins

By early 1947, people started moving based
on their religious affiliations. Muslims in Hindu-
majority areas began heading towards regions
expected to be part of Pakistan, while Hindus and
Sikhs in Muslim-majority areas did the same in the
opposite direction. This migration was
accompanied by uncertainty and fear.

Economic and Social Disruptions

The impending division caused severe
economic uncertainty. Businesses were shut down,

properties were abandoned, and supply chains were disrupted. Additionally, the social fabric of mixed communities began unraveling as long-time neighbors turned against each other.

Violence and Breakdown of Order

Throughout 1947, communal riots escalated in Punjab, Bengal, and other parts of India. British authorities, overwhelmed by the scale of violence, failed to maintain law and order. The collapse of governance led to massacres, forced conversions, abductions, and sexual violence, marking one of the darkest periods in South Asian history.

The Demand for Pakistan and the Lahore Resolution (1940)

The Lahore Resolution, passed by the Muslim League on March 23, 1940, was a defining moment in the struggle for Pakistan. It called for independent states for Muslims in the northwestern and eastern parts of India, setting the stage for the formal demand for partition. Sindh was one of the first provinces to endorse this resolution, reflecting the growing sentiment among Sindhi Muslims for a separate nation.

The Influence of Sindhi Muslim Leaders

Sindhi leaders like G. M. Syed played a pivotal role in rallying support for the Pakistan movement. Syed, initially a Congress supporter, became one of the most vocal proponents of Pakistan, aligning with Jinnah's vision. His efforts helped consolidate Muslim League support in

Sindh, making it a stronghold for the demand for
Pakistan.

3. Communal Tensions and the 1946 Elections

The 1946 elections were a watershed
moment, with the Muslim League securing a
decisive victory in Sindh. This victory underscored
the growing division between Hindus and Muslims
in the province. The League's success fueled Hindu
apprehensions, leading to heightened communal
anxieties and sporadic clashes.

The Role of Communal Riots

By the mid-1940s, India was witnessing an
increase in communal riots. Sindh, though initially
less affected, eventually succumbed to these
tensions. The violence in places like Karachi and
Hyderabad signaled the breakdown of communal
harmony and reinforced the urgency of partition.

4. British Policies and the Final Steps Toward Partition

As Britain prepared to withdraw from India,
the political negotiations between the Indian
National Congress, the Muslim League, and British
authorities became increasingly fraught. Lord
Mountbatten, the last Viceroy of India, proposed a
plan for the partition of India, which was
reluctantly accepted by all parties.

The Impact on Sindh

Sindh, with its significant Hindu
population, faced profound consequences. Many

Sindhi Hindus, fearing persecution, began migrating to India, leaving behind their ancestral homes and businesses. Conversely, Sindh became a primary destination for Muslim refugees from other parts of India, drastically altering its demographic and cultural landscape.

5. The Aftermath: Refugee Crisis and Cultural Shifts

The partition resulted in one of the largest mass migrations in history, with millions displaced. Sindh became home to an influx of Muhajirs (Muslim migrants from India), reshaping its urban centres and social dynamics. The migration also led to the loss of Sindh's Hindu elite, who had played a crucial role in trade, education, and administration.

4. Conclusion

The call for partition was fuel by deep-seated political, social, and religious divisions that had been exacerbated by colonial rule and competing nationalist visions. The events leading up to partition—political confrontations, communal violence, and economic disruptions—foreshadowed the immense human tragedy that would unfold in August 1947. The early signs of displacement, visible in the years leading up to partition, only intensified as borders were drawn, leading to one of the largest forced migrations in history, with millions uprooted from their homes.

While partition created two sovereign nations, India and Pakistan, its legacy remains deeply ingrained in the collective memory of the subcontinent. The violence, displacement, and trauma it inflicted continue to shape Indo-Pak relations and the socio-political landscape of South Asia to this day.

Summary

The Call for Partition: Political Turmoil and Rising Tensions

The call for partition was not merely a political maneuver but a manifestation of deep-seated historical, social, and religious divisions that had festered over decades. The rising tensions in the Indian subcontinent during the early to mid-20th century were the result of conflicting nationalisms, the inability of political leaders to reach a sustainable compromise, and the colonial policy of divide and rule. While the demand for partition was rooted in the desire for self-determination, it also led to one of the most traumatic events in South Asian history—the division of India and the creation of Pakistan in 1947.

One of the key aspects of this political turmoil was the growing mistrust between the Indian National Congress and the All-India Muslim League. The League, under the leadership of Muhammad Ali Jinnah, argued that Muslims were a distinct nation with their own cultural, religious, and political identity, necessitating a separate homeland. On the other hand, the Congress, led by leaders like Mahatma Gandhi and Jawaharlal Nehru, envisioned a united India where all communities could coexist. However, repeated failures in negotiations, including the breakdown of the Cabinet Mission Plan, deepened the divide and made partition appear inevitable.

The communal tensions escalated into widespread violence, especially after the Lahore Resolution of 1940, which formally demanded a separate Muslim state. As independence drew closer, riots, massacres, and mass migrations turned the subcontinent into a landscape of chaos and suffering. The Radcliffe Line, hastily drawn to demarcate the borders between India and Pakistan, led to widespread displacement, with millions of Hindus, Muslims, and Sikhs forced to abandon their homes. This large-scale migration resulted in one of the largest humanitarian crises of the 20th century, with an estimated one to two million people losing their lives due to communal violence, starvation, and disease.

Beyond the immediate humanitarian catastrophe, the legacy of partition continues to shape South Asia's political landscape. The bitter memories of the division have fueled tensions between India and Pakistan, leading to multiple wars and a persistent state of hostility. The unresolved issue of Kashmir, a direct consequence of partition, remains a major flashpoint in Indo-Pakistani relations, further complicating diplomatic efforts. Additionally, within both nations, partition left deep scars in their respective social fabrics, with religious and ethnic divisions continuing to influence politics and society.

Despite the suffering it caused, partition also had significant historical consequences. It led to the emergence of two independent nations, each pursuing its own path in governance, economy, and international relations. While India embraced secular democracy, Pakistan initially adopted a mix of democracy and military rule, shaping distinct national identities. The event also reshaped migration patterns, economic structures, and the cultural narratives of millions of people who lived through it.

In retrospect, partition stands as a stark reminder of the dangers of political polarization, communalism, and the failure to accommodate diverse identities within a single national framework. It highlights the consequences of short-sighted political decisions and the devastating impact of forced migration and sectarian violence. While India and Pakistan have made significant strides since their independence, the echoes of partition still influence their socio-political dynamics.

As history continues to unfold, the lessons from partition remain relevant in contemporary global politics. The need for dialogue, mutual understanding, and coexistence is more important than ever to prevent similar conflicts in other parts of the world. While the wounds of partition may never fully heal, acknowledging its history and learning from its mistakes can pave the way for a more peaceful and cooperative future between India, Pakistan, and the broader South Asian region.

Chapter 4

The Role of Women in Sindhi Society

Women in Sindhi society have historically played a vital role in shaping the cultural, social, and economic fabric of the region. Despite facing traditional constraints, they have consistently exhibited resilience, adaptability, and strength. Their contributions span from domestic responsibilities to leadership in various fields, making them an integral part of Sindhi civilization.

Sindhi culture, deeply rooted in traditions, has long upheld the reverence of women as the custodians of family values and heritage. In traditional settings, women have been central to maintaining the household, raising children, and passing down cultural values through generations. They have preserved folklore, cuisine, language, and rituals that define Sindhi identity. However, their role is not confined to domestic spheres alone; Sindhi women have historically been active in trade, agriculture, and artisanal crafts, contributing significantly to the local economy.

Education has been a transformative force in redefining women's roles in Sindhi society. In contemporary times, Sindhi women have increasingly accessed higher education and professional careers. Many have excelled in academia, politics, medicine, and business, breaking stereotypes and paving the way for future generations. The progress in female literacy and awareness campaigns has played a crucial role in empowering women to participate more actively in decision-making processes within families and communities.

Sindhi women have also made their mark in social and political spheres. Several have emerged as influential leaders advocating for women's rights, social reforms, and economic empowerment. Their participation in grassroots movements and non-governmental organizations (NGOs) has led to significant strides in gender equality and social justice. Women's involvement in policymaking and governance has further strengthened their agency in Sindhi society, demonstrating their capability to lead and inspire change.

Despite these advancements, challenges remain. Issues such as gender discrimination, economic disparities, and conservative social norms continue to hinder the full realization of women's potential in Sindhi society. Many women still struggle for equal opportunities in education, employment, and leadership roles. Early marriages, limited financial independence, and patriarchal traditions persist in some rural and traditional households. However, awareness and legal frameworks are progressively addressing these challenges, offering hope for a more equitable future.

The resilience and adaptability of Sindhi women highlight their ability to balance tradition and modernity. While they continue to uphold cultural values, they are also embracing contemporary roles that demand independence, creativity, and leadership. The evolving role of women in Sindhi society serves as a testament to their enduring strength and the community's gradual acceptance of gender equality.

In conclusion, women in Sindhi society are not merely passive bearers of tradition but active agents of change. Their contributions across various sectors demonstrate their indispensable role in the progress of Sindh. As education, awareness, and legal reforms continue to advance gender equality, the future holds immense promise for Sindhi women. By fostering inclusivity and empowering women, Sindhi society can ensure a more prosperous, balanced, and progressive community where both men and women thrive together.

Chapter 5

Sindh's Economic and Business Legacy: The Entrepreneurial Spirit of Sindhis

Introduction

Sindh, a land steeped in history, has long been a hub of economic activity and entrepreneurial brilliance. From the ancient trade routes of the Indus Valley Civilization to the bustling markets of modern Karachi, the region has nurtured a thriving business culture. The Sindhi community, known for its adaptability and commercial acumen, has played a vital role in shaping the economic fabric of Sindh and beyond. This chapter explores the economic and business legacy of Sindh, highlighting the entrepreneurial spirit, traditional trade practices, and modern enterprises that define its commercial landscape.

The Ancient Economic Landscape of Sindh

Sindh's economic history dates back over 4,500 years to the Indus Valley Civilization, one of the world's earliest urban societies. The cities of Mohenjo-daro and Harappa were centers of commerce, engaging in extensive trade with Mesopotamia, Persia, and Central Asia. Archaeological findings reveal a well-planned economic system based on agriculture, handicrafts, and a sophisticated barter trade network. The region's strategic location along the Indus River facilitated the movement of goods, laying the foundation for Sindh's mercantile tradition.

Sindhi Traders and the Silk Route

During the medieval period, Sindh emerged as a vital trading center on the Silk Route, connecting South Asia with Central Asia, the Middle East, and Europe. The Sindhi traders, known for their maritime expertise, established commercial links with distant lands, exporting textiles, spices, and handicrafts. The ports of Debal and Thatta became significant trading hubs, attracting merchants from Persia, Arabia, and Africa. The success of Sindhi traders was rooted in their ability to navigate the complexities of cross-border trade, mastering multiple languages, and understanding diverse market dynamics.

The British Era and the Expansion of Sindhi Business Networks

The advent of British colonial rule in the 19th century brought new economic opportunities and challenges to Sindh. The construction of the Sukkur Barrage and extensive railway networks facilitated trade and agriculture. Sindhi entrepreneurs capitalized on these developments, expanding their businesses beyond Sindh to Bombay, Calcutta, and even Southeast Asia and Africa. The British era also saw the rise of Sindhi banking families and trading houses, which played a crucial role in financing trade and industrial activities.

The Partition and the Global Sindhi Diaspora

The Partition of India in 1947 forced many Sindhis to migrate, leading to the emergence of a dynamic Sindhi diaspora across India, the Middle East, Africa, and beyond. Despite losing their homeland, Sindhis quickly rebuilt their commercial empire, excelling in sectors such as textiles, electronics, and real estate. The resilience and adaptability of Sindhi entrepreneurs became evident as they established thriving businesses in new environments, continuing their centuries-old legacy of trade and enterprise.

Traditional Business Practices of Sindhis

Sindhi business culture is characterized by unique practices that have been passed down through generations. Some of the core principles include:

1. Risk-taking and Adaptability: Sindhi traders have historically ventured into uncharted markets, taking calculated risks to expand their businesses.

2. Family-Owned Enterprises: Many Sindhi businesses operate as family-run establishments, ensuring continuity and trust in business dealings.

3. Community Networks and Trust: The Sindhi community relies heavily on trust-based transactions and informal financial systems, such as the hundi system, to facilitate trade.

4. Customer-Centric Approach: Sindhi entrepreneurs emphasize long-term customer relationships, often prioritizing reliability over short-term profits.

The Modern Business Landscape in Sindh

In contemporary times, Sindh continues to be a major economic hub, with Karachi serving as Pakistan's financial capital. The province hosts key industries such as textiles, manufacturing, information technology, and finance. Major business groups, such as the Hashwani Group and the House of Habib, have their roots in Sindh and have expanded their reach globally. The Karachi Stock Exchange, one of South Asia's most active financial markets, further underscores Sindh's economic significance.

Challenges and Future Prospects

Despite its rich economic heritage, Sindh faces several challenges, including political instability, corruption, and infrastructural deficits. However, the entrepreneurial spirit of Sindhis remains undeterred. The rise of e-commerce, fintech, and startup culture in Karachi indicates a shift towards innovation-driven enterprises. Government initiatives aimed at improving ease of doing business and investment-friendly policies offer hope for sustained economic growth.

Conclusion

The economic and business legacy of Sindh is a testament to the resilience, ingenuity, and enterprising nature of its people. From ancient trade networks to modern multinational enterprises, Sindhis have consistently demonstrated their ability to adapt and thrive in diverse economic environments. As Sindh continues to evolve, its entrepreneurial spirit remains a driving force, ensuring that its legacy as a commercial powerhouse endures for generations to come.

Chapter 6

The Great Migration Stories of Departure and Heartbreak

Migration has long been a defining force in human history—shaping civilizations, economies, and cultures. But behind every movement lies a deeply personal story of departure, loss, and survival. Whether driven by war, famine, climate change, or the search for a better future, migration is rarely a choice made lightly. It is an upheaval, a fracture from the familiar, and often a journey fraught with chaos and danger.

From the desperate crossings of deserts and seas to the silent struggles of those left behind, the path of migration is marked by uncertainty and resilience. Families are torn apart, identities are reshaped, and survival becomes a relentless battle. Some find refuge, while others face hostility and rejection. For many, the journey is not just a physical displacement but an emotional and psychological transformation—one that tests the limits of human endurance.

This chapter delves into the heart-wrenching narratives of migration, exploring the sacrifices, hopes, and sheer resilience of those who leave everything behind in pursuit of safety or opportunity. It brings to light the voices often lost in history—the refugees fleeing war zones, the laborers exploited in foreign lands, the generations displaced by political upheavals, and the children forced to grow up too soon.

Through these stories of departure and heartbreak, we come to understand migration not just as a movement of people but as a testament to human strength, survival, and the universal longing for home.

Story 1-

Kewal Ram: A Journey of Resilience and Triumph

In the turbulent days of Partition, countless families were forced to abandon their homes and embark on uncertain journeys to rebuild their lives. Among them was a seven-year-old boy named Kewal Ram, who left Sindh with his parents and seven siblings. Their life in Sindh had been comfortable, with a thriving family business that provided them a stable and prosperous lifestyle. However, as they crossed the border into newly independent India, they arrived with nothing—no money, no possessions, only the weight of their past and the hope for a better future.

Struggles in a New Land

Settling in an unfamiliar country with no financial security was an immense challenge. Kewal Ram's father, once a successful businessman, was now left with no choice but to take up a job in a cloth shop. Though he worked tirelessly, his earnings were barely enough to feed the large family. The burden of poverty fell heavily upon them, forcing Kewal Ram's two eldest brothers to make a heartbreaking sacrifice—they gave up their education to work in a shop and contribute to the household income.

As Kewal Ram grew older, he too felt the weight of responsibility on his small shoulders. Determined to support his family while continuing his education, he took up small part-time jobs. Balancing work and studies were exhausting, but he remained steadfast in his resolve. He understood that only perseverance and hard work could pull his family out of poverty.

The Road to Prosperity

Years of struggle eventually began to bear fruit. The brothers, having gained experience in the trade, decided to take a leap of faith. Pooling their limited resources, they started a small cloth shop of their own. The business grew slowly at first, but with their collective dedication and unwavering determination, it soon flourished. What began as a modest shop quickly expanded into a thriving enterprise, a testament to their resilience and hard work.

Success, however, did not change the values that had kept them going through the darkest times. Even as they prospered, they remained humble and grateful for the journey that had shaped them.

A Life of Fulfillment and Giving Back

With financial stability finally within their grasp, the family was able to turn their attention to personal milestones. Kewal Ram's brothers and sisters were married, and eventually, he too found companionship in a loving and supportive wife. Together, they built a life of happiness, ensuring that their children received the education and opportunities they had once struggled to attain.

However, Kewal Ram never forgot his past. Remembering the hardships of his childhood, he and his brothers made it their mission to give back to society. They began supporting underprivileged students, offering financial aid for education and ensuring that others would not have to endure the struggles they had faced. Through scholarships and charitable contributions, they helped countless young minds shape a brighter future.

The Legacy of Kewal Ram

Kewal Ram's journey was one of resilience, sacrifice, and ultimate triumph. From a helpless refugee boy to a successful businessman and philanthropist, his story is a beacon of hope and inspiration. His life serves as a powerful reminder that even in the face of the greatest adversities, perseverance and kindness can pave the way for a better future.

Today, the legacy of Kewal Ram and his family lives on—not just in their flourishing business, but in the many lives they have touched through their generosity and compassion. Their story stands as a testament to the unbreakable spirit of those who refuse to be defeated by circumstances, proving that true success is not just measured by wealth, but by the impact one leaves on the world.

Story -2

Lachman Das: A Journey of Resilience and Compassion

In the sweltering summer of 1947, the air was thick with uncertainty and fear as millions of people were uprooted from their homes in the wake of Partition. Among them was a ten-year-old boy named Lachman Das, who clung to his mother's hand as their family left behind everything they had known in undivided India. With his parents and four sisters, he embarked on a journey into the unknown, carrying only memories of a home that was no longer theirs. They had no idea what lay ahead, only that they had to survive.

The Struggle of a New Beginning

Upon arriving in independent India, life was anything but easy. The family moved from place to place, searching for stability. Their journey took them from Sagar to Ujjain, then to Pilibhit in Uttar Pradesh, before they finally settled in Bhopal. With each move came new challenges—poverty, uncertainty, and the struggle to rebuild a life from scratch. Yet, despite the hardships, young Lachman Das refused to let despair take root in his heart.

His father, once a man of dignity and stability, now worked as a laborer in a private job to sustain his family. Seeing his father's struggles, Lachman Das decided that he, too, had to contribute. At a young age, he took up a small job alongside his father, earning whatever he could to help put food on the table. However, he was determined not to let his circumstances dictate his future—education remained his priority. Balancing work and studies were no easy feat, but Lachman Das persevered, studying under the dim glow of a lantern after long hours of labor.

Sacrifices and Responsibilities

As the eldest son, responsibility weighed heavily on his shoulders. The first priority for Lachman Das was ensuring the well-being of his family. With immense dedication and selflessness, he worked tirelessly to support his four sisters. He made sure that each of them was married into respectable families before thinking about his own future. His sacrifices were not unnoticed—his family admired his strength and resilience, and his unwavering commitment to their happiness.

Only after securing his sisters' futures did Lachman Das think about his own life. He got married to a kind-hearted woman who shared his values and dreams. She became his pillar of support, standing beside him as he navigated the challenges of building a better future.

Building a Business from Scratch

Despite his circumstances, Lachman Das never let go of his dreams. He had always been an ambitious and hardworking man, determined to break free from the cycle of poverty. With years of experience working in different jobs and an acute understanding of business, he decided to take a leap of faith—he started his own manufacturing company.

It was not an easy journey. With limited resources, setting up the business required immense effort, persistence, and patience. There were days when finances were tight, and setbacks threatened to crush his hopes. But Lachman Das was not one to back down. Through sheer dedication and hard work, his business slowly began to grow. The small manufacturing unit expanded, gaining recognition for its quality and reliability. His enterprise flourished, and before long, he became a successful businessman.

Yet, success did not change him. He remained the same humble, compassionate man who once struggled to make ends meet. He knew what it meant to suffer, and he never forgot those who were still struggling.

A Life of Giving Back

For Lachman Das, wealth was not just about personal prosperity—it was a means to uplift others. He had experienced poverty firsthand, and he knew the pain of being denied opportunities due to financial constraints. Determined to make a difference, he devoted a significant portion of his resources to social causes.

One of his biggest contributions was in the field of education. He firmly believed that education was the key to breaking the cycle of poverty. To ensure that financial struggles did not hinder anyone's dreams, he established schools and colleges with minimal fees, making quality education accessible to all. His institutions welcomed children from underprivileged backgrounds, giving them a chance at a brighter future. Many students who once had no hope of education found new possibilities because of Lachman Das's generosity.

His philanthropic efforts extended beyond education. Whether it was providing financial aid to struggling families, supporting orphans, or helping small businesses grow, Lachman Das was always ready to lend a helping hand. His acts of kindness made him a beloved figure in the community—a businessman with a heart of gold.

The Legacy of Lachman Das

Lachman Das's journey from a displaced ten-year-old refugee to a successful businessman and a revered social worker was nothing short of extraordinary. His story was one of resilience, sacrifice, and an unwavering belief in the power of hard work. But more than that, it was a testament to the strength of the human spirit—the ability to rise from nothing and build not just a prosperous life for oneself, but also a legacy of generosity and kindness.

Through his struggles, he learned that success was not just about achieving personal wealth, but about uplifting those around him. His schools and colleges continue to educate thousands, his businesses provide employment to many, and his philanthropic efforts inspire generations.

Even today, the name Lachman Das is remembered not just as a successful entrepreneur, but as a beacon of hope for those who dare to dream despite the odds. His life stands as a reminder that no matter how difficult the journey, with perseverance, selflessness, and a heart full of compassion, one can turn hardships into a story of triumph.

His legacy lives on, not just in the businesses he built or the institutions he founded, but in the countless lives he touched and the spirit of generosity he instilled in others. Lachman Das was not just a refugee who rebuilt his life—he was a guiding light for many, proving that true success lies in lifting others as you rise.

Story 3

Koshi and Pritam: A Journey of Love, Sacrifice, and Service

Koshi was a young woman full of dreams, married to Pritam, a well-educated and kind-hearted man who held a respected government job. Pritam's family-owned vast acres of land, ensuring a comfortable life for them. However, despite the stability and security that surrounded them, Pritam's heart was drawn to a cause much greater than personal success—the struggle for India's independence. Deeply influenced by Mahatma Gandhi's ideals of non-violence and selfless service, he soon found himself at the forefront of the freedom movement.

Koshi admired her husband's unwavering commitment to justice, but she also feared for their future. The British government was harsh on those who opposed their rule, and the thought of losing Pritam to imprisonment or worse was unbearable. Yet, she knew that his heart burned with a passion for his motherland. With a silent prayer and immense strength, she supported his decision, choosing to stand by him through the uncertainties of revolution.

As Pritam plunged deeper into the movement, he participated in protests, led campaigns promoting self-reliance, and helped spread awareness about the power of unity. Koshi, too, found herself becoming a part of this silent revolution. Though she was not on the streets protesting, she played her role in inspiring and motivating other women to stand strong. She ensured their home remained a place of refuge for those fighting for the cause, often feeding and sheltering freedom fighters who needed a safe space to rest.

Then came the dark days of Partition. Sindh, the land they had called home for generations, was no longer safe for Hindus. The riots, chaos, and political turmoil forced Pritam and Koshi to make the most difficult decision of their lives—to leave their homeland and move to India. With a heavy heart, they packed whatever little they could carry and joined thousands of others on a journey filled with uncertainty.

The journey to divided India was arduous. They witnessed the pain of people losing their families, homes, and identities overnight. But amid the despair, Pritam held on to his resolve. He believed that though they had lost their land, they had not lost their purpose. Arriving in India as refugees, they faced days of hardship, struggling to find shelter and rebuild their lives from scratch. Yet, Koshi and Pritam never lost hope.

While many who had been displaced struggled to regain financial stability, Pritam took a different path. Instead of returning to his government job, he chose to pursue his dream of becoming a doctor. With Koshi's unwavering support, he completed his further studies in medicine, dedicating himself to serving those who had suffered due to Partition. He set up a small clinic in a refugee camp, treating the sick and injured without demanding payment. For him, medicine was not just a profession—it was a means to heal a wounded nation.

Koshi stood by him every step of the way, managing their modest home and assisting him in his medical endeavours. She comforted grieving families, helped displaced women rebuild their lives, and ensured that no one left their doorstep hungry. Though she never wore the title of a freedom fighter, she was a warrior in her own right—a woman who turned personal loss into a beacon of hope for others.

Years passed, and Pritam's selfless service earned him great respect in the community. People no longer saw him as just a doctor; they saw him as a saviour, a man who had dedicated his life to humanity. Koshi, too, became a figure of strength and compassion, an inspiration to many women who had once thought they had no future.

Together, they proved that true fulfillment does not lie in wealth or power but in the service of others. Koshi and Pritam's journey—from a prosperous life in Sindh to becoming refugees and then transforming into pillars of their community—was a testament to the power of resilience, sacrifice, and love.

As the years went by, their story became one of legend, narrated to younger generations as a reminder of what it means to live for a cause greater than oneself. Their love for each other and their devotion to their people remained eternal, proving that even in the face of loss and displacement, hope and purpose can light the way forward.

Chapter 7

Conclusion: The Everlasting Legacy of Sindh

Sindh, a land of ancient wisdom, resilience, and cultural vibrancy, has stood as a witness to the tides of time. From the banks of the Indus River to the sprawling urban centres, this region has been an epicentre of civilization, trade, and intellectual growth. The narrative of Sindh is not merely a collection of historical events but a living testament to human endurance, adaptability, and progress. As we conclude this journey through Sindh's past and present, it is crucial to reflect on the essence of what makes Sindh truly remarkable—the struggles, the triumphs, and the aspirations of its people.

Sindh's Rich Cultural and Geographical Significance

Sindh's geographical landscape, defined by the Indus River, has shaped its identity for millennia. The region's fertile lands supported one of the earliest civilizations—the Indus Valley Civilization—whose contributions to urban planning, trade, and governance continue to intrigue historians and archaeologists. Over the centuries, Sindh became a melting pot of cultures, influenced by Persian, Arab, Central Asian, and British forces. Despite these influences, Sindh retained its unique identity, deeply rooted in Sufism, poetry, music, and a communal spirit that transcends religious and ethnic divisions.

The cultural wealth of Sindh is exemplified by its literary and artistic traditions. The works of Shah Abdul Latif Bhittai, Sachal Sarmast, and others reflect the deep spiritual and humanistic ethos of the Sindhi people. The region's music and folklore, infused with themes of love, devotion, and resilience, continue to inspire generations. Even as modernity seeps into Sindh's urban landscapes, the heart of Sindh beats with the rhythm of its historical traditions, ensuring that its heritage is not lost but rather evolves with time.

The Impact of Partition: A Struggle for Identity and Belonging

The Partition of 1947 was a turning point in Sindh's history, marking a profound shift in its demographic, economic, and political landscape. Unlike Punjab and Bengal, where violence was immediate and widespread, Sindh experienced a more gradual transformation. The migration of Hindus, who had played a significant role in Sindh's economic and social fabric, created a void that took decades to fill. Meanwhile, the influx of Muhajirs from India reshaped the cultural dynamics of Sindh, leading to tensions and the need for new social adjustments.

The struggle for identity has remained a defining feature of post-Partition Sindh. The rise of Sindhi nationalism, efforts to preserve the Sindhi language, and the political movements advocating for the rights of Sindh's indigenous population highlight the ongoing quest to maintain a distinct Sindhi ethos within the broader framework of Pakistan. The balance between preserving cultural identity and embracing the evolving national narrative continues to challenge policymakers and cultural activists alike.

Women's Education and Empowerment: A Road Paved with Challenges and Triumphs

Women in Sindh have long played a pivotal role in the region's cultural and economic spheres, yet their struggle for education and empowerment has been fraught with challenges. Historically, social and religious constraints limited women's access to education, but the tide began to shift in the 20th century with the establishment of educational institutions dedicated to female literacy. Today, Sindh boasts numerous universities and colleges that cater to women, fostering a new generation of empowered individuals determined to shape their futures.

Despite these advancements, gender disparity remains a pressing issue. Rural areas, in particular, still grapple with traditional mindsets that hinder female education and economic participation. However, initiatives led by activists, NGOs, and government programs have steadily improved literacy rates and professional opportunities for women. The growing presence of Sindhi women in politics, academia, entrepreneurship, and activism signifies a shift towards greater inclusivity and equality.

Business and Economic Growth: The Evolution of Sindh's Economic Landscape

Sindh has historically been a commercial hub, benefiting from its strategic location and access to global trade routes. The port city of Karachi, often termed the 'economic backbone of Pakistan,' drives the nation's economy through its industries, financial institutions, and international trade. The region's agricultural sector, supported by the Indus River, continues to be a major contributor to Pakistan's food supply and exports.

However, economic disparities between urban and rural Sindh remain stark. While Karachi thrives as a modern metropolis, rural areas struggle with issues such as inadequate infrastructure, water scarcity, and limited industrialization. The need for equitable economic policies that bridge this gap is paramount. Investments in technology, sustainable agriculture, and infrastructure development could unlock Sindh's full economic potential, ensuring prosperity for all segments of society.

The Future of Sindh: A Vision for Progress and Unity

As Sindh navigates the complexities of the 21st century, its future rests on a delicate balance of preserving heritage while embracing modernity. The challenges of political instability, environmental degradation, and economic inequality must be addressed through sustainable policies and inclusive governance.

A key aspect of Sindh's progress lies in its youth. With increasing access to education, digital resources, and global connectivity, the younger generation holds the power to drive transformative change. Promoting innovation, entrepreneurship, and cultural preservation will be instrumental in shaping a progressive Sindh that remains deeply connected to its roots while forging ahead into a promising future.

The legacy of Sindh is not confined to its past but is continuously being written by those who inhabit it today. Whether through the resilience of its people, the wisdom of its poets, or the aspirations of its youth, Sindh continues to stand as a beacon of cultural and historical significance. As we conclude this exploration of Sindh, we recognize that its story is far from over—it is an ever-evolving

narrative of strength, unity, and an unbreakable
spirit.

About Author

Dr. Jahanavi Ahuja, a native of Bhopal, Madhya Pradesh, and now a resident of Betul, is a woman of many passions. Her academic pursuits, including an M Sc, M.A, B.Ed., and a Ph.D. in English Literature, are a testament to her dedication and intellectual prowess. As a loving mother of two teenagers, she brings the same enthusiasm to her roles as a homemaker and an avid blogger. Her articles have graced the pages of various newspapers. With the publication of this book, she further cemented her status as a prolific author, having written extensively on non-fiction topics for several years.

For the past few years, Dr. Jahanavi Ahuja has been on a mission to empower women through yoga. Her dedication to this ancient discipline has led her to teach yoga to hundreds of individuals, focusing on women. She conducts both in-person and online sessions, tailoring her classes to suit the needs of women at various stages of life. She imparts physical practices through these sessions and emphasizes mental and emotional well-being. Her approach has gained a significant following as she creates a supportive community where participants can connect, learn, and grow in their yoga journey.

Dr. Jahanavi Ahuja is widely recognized for her commitment to empowering women, a cause she passionately champions through her writing and teaching. Her dedication to this pursuit is reflected in her work, particularly in her internationally acclaimed books.

1. Wonder Women

'In Wonder Woman', Dr. Ahuja explores the strength, resilience, and unique challenges women face today. It delves into inspirational stories of women who have overcome adversities and shattered societal expectations to reach the pinnacle of success in various fields. Through these stories, she motivates readers to embrace their inner strength and encourages them to lead confidently and purposefully. The book, with its global resonance, celebrates the power and potential of women across cultures, inspiring a worldwide movement of empowerment.

Link to book:

https://relinks.me/B0983QH2BF

2. Women With Will & Wings

In Women 'With Will & Wings', Dr. Ahuja continues her exploration of women's empowerment, focusing on the importance of self-determination and courage in the face of challenges. The book highlights the journey of women who, with sheer willpower and determination, have transformed their lives, defying odds and societal norms. Each narrative is a testament to the unyielding spirit of women, offering readers not just inspiration, but also practical insights that can be applied to overcome personal and professional hurdles.

Link to book

https://relinks.me/B094H8CPH5

3. Master Yoga Bliss

Master Yoga Bliss is an inspiring guide to healing and transformation through yoga. Sharing her journey from chronic pain to peace, the author—a mother, PhD scholar, and yoga therapist—reveals how mindful movement restored her well-being. This book offers practical techniques for pain relief, stress management, and self-awareness, making the ancient practice of yoga accessible to all. With step-by-step guidance on restorative poses, breathing exercises, and mindfulness practices, readers can cultivate balance, resilience, and holistic healing. **Master Yoga Bliss** is more than a yoga manual—it's a path to self-care, empowerment, and a healthier, more harmonious life.

Link to book

https://relinks.me/B0DHH11CJ4

4. Master Mindful Meditation

Master Mindful Meditation is a transformative guide to integrating mindfulness into daily life, making meditation a welcoming practice for everyone. Whether you're a beginner or an experienced practitioner, this book is designed to simplify meditation and offer practical steps to cultivate mental clarity, emotional balance, and inner peace. It explores the benefits of mindfulness, from reducing stress and anxiety to enhancing focus and well-being. Readers will discover meditation techniques, including breath awareness, body scans, and loving-kindness practices. Through real-life success stories and scientific insights, this book empowers individuals to embrace mindfulness, fostering resilience, self-growth, and a more fulfilling, present-centered life.

Link to book

https://relinks.me/B0DMPCXZG5

These titles have garnered international recognition and solidified Dr. Ahuja's reputation as a thought leader in women's empowerment through her writing, she continues to inspire and uplift women, encouraging them to embrace their potential and soar to new heights.